Of Building

Francis Bacon

Kessinger Publishing's Rare Reprints

Thousands of Scarce and Hard-to-Find Books on These and other Subjects!

- Americana
- Ancient Mysteries
- Animals
- Anthropology
- Architecture
- Arts
- Astrology
- Bibliographies
- Biographies & Memoirs
- Body, Mind & Spirit
- Business & Investing
- Children & Young Adult
- Collectibles
- Comparative Religions
- Crafts & Hobbies
- Earth Sciences
- Education
- Ephemera
- Fiction
- Folklore
- Geography
- Health & Diet
- History
- Hobbies & Leisure
- Humor
- Illustrated Books
- Language & Culture
- Law
- Life Sciences
- Literature
- Medicine & Pharmacy
- Metaphysical
- Music
- Mystery & Crime
- Mythology
- Natural History
- Outdoor & Nature
- Philosophy
- Poetry
- Political Science
- Science
- Psychiatry & Psychology
- Reference
- Religion & Spiritualism
- Rhetoric
- Sacred Books
- Science Fiction
- Science & Technology
- Self-Help
- Social Sciences
- Symbolism
- Theatre & Drama
- Theology
- Travel & Explorations
- War & Military
- Women
- Yoga
- *Plus Much More!*

We kindly invite you to view our catalog list at:
http://www.kessinger.net

XLV.—OF BUILDING

HOUSES are built to live in, and not to look on ; therefore
let use be preferred before uniformity, except where both
may be had. Leave the goodly fabrics of houses, for
beauty only, to the enchanted palaces of the poets, who
build them with small cost. He that builds a fair house
upon an ill seat, * committeth himself to prison : neither
do I reckon it an ill seat only where the air is unwholesome,
but likewise where the air is unequal ; as you shall see
many fine seats set upon a knap † of ground, environed
with higher hills round about it, whereby the heat of
the sun is pent in, and the wind gathereth as in troughs ;
so as you shall have, and that suddenly, as great diversity
of heat and cold as if you dwelt in several places. Neither
is it ill air only that maketh an ill seat ; but ill ways, ill
markets, and, if you will consult with Momus, ‡ ill neigh-
bours. I speak not of many more ; want of water,
want of wood, shade, and shelter, want of fruitfulness,
and mixture of grounds of several natures ; want of
prospect, want of level grounds, want of places at some
near distance for sports of hunting, hawking, and races ;
too near the sea, too remote ; having the commodity
of navigable rivers, or the discommodity of their over-
flowing ; too far off from great cities, which may hinder
business ; or too near them, which lurcheth § all pro-
visions, and maketh everything dear ; where a man
hath a great living laid together ; and where he is scanted ;
all which, as it is impossible perhaps to find together, so
it is good to know them, and think of them, that a man
may take as many as he can ; and if he have several
dwellings, that he sort them so, that what he wanteth

* Site.   † Knoll.
‡ Have a liking for cheerful society, Momus being the god of
mirth.   § Eats up.

in the one he may find in the other. Lucullus answered Pompey well, who, when he saw his stately galleries and rooms so large and lightsome, in one of his houses, said, *Surely an excellent place for summer, but how do you in winter?* Lucullus answered, *Why, do you not think me as wise as some fowls are, that ever change their abode towards the winter?*

To pass from the seat to the house itself, we will do as Cicero doth in the orator's art, who writes books De Oratore, and a book he entitles Orator; whereof the former delivers the precepts of the art, and the latter the perfection. We will therefore describe a princely palace, making a brief model thereof; for it is strange to see, now in Europe, such huge buildings as the Vatican and Escurial, and some others be, and yet scarce a very fair room in them.

First, therefore, I say, you cannot have a perfect palace, except you have two several sides; a side for the banquet, as is spoken of in the book of Esther,* and a side for the household; the one for feasts and triumphs, and the other for dwelling. I understand both these sides to be not only returns, but parts of the front; and to be uniform without, though severally partitioned within; and to be on both sides of a great and stately tower in the midst of the front, that as it were joineth them together on either hand. I would have, on the side of the banquet in front, one only goodly room above stairs, of some forty foot high; and under it a room for a dressing or preparing place, at times of triumphs. On the other side, which is the household side, I wish it divided at the first into a hall and a chapel (with a partition between), both of good state and big-ness; and those not to go all the length, but to have at the further end a winter and a summer parlour, both fair; and under these rooms a fair and large cellar

* Esther i. 5.

sunk under ground; and likewise some privy kitchens, with butteries and pantries, and the like. As for the tower, I would have it two stories, of eighteen foot high apiece above the two wings; and a goodly leads upon the top, railed with statues interposed; and the same tower to be divided into rooms, as shall be thought fit, The stairs likewise to the upper rooms, let them be upon a fair open newel, * and finely railed in with images of wood cast into a brass colour; and a very fair landing-place at the top. But this to be, if you do not point any of the lower rooms for a dining-place of servants; for, otherwise, you shall have the servants' dinner after your own : for the steam of it will come up as in a tunnel. † And so much for the front : only I understand the height of the first stairs to be sixteen foot, which is the height of the lower room.

Beyond this front is there to be a fair court, but three sides of it of a far lower building than the front; and in all the four corners of that court fair staircases, cast into turrets on the outside, and not within the row of buildings themselves : but those towers are not to be of the height of the front, but rather proportionable to the lower building. Let the court not be paved, for that striketh up a great heat in summer, and much cold in winter : but only some side alleys with a cross, and the quarters to graze, being kept shorn, but not too near shorn. The row of return on the banquet side, let it be all stately galleries : in which galleries let there be three or five fine cupolas in the length of it, placed at equal distance, and fine coloured windows of several works : on the household side, chambers of presence and ordinary entertainments, with some bed-chambers : and let all three sides be a double house, without thorough

* The cylinder formed by the small end of the steps of winding stairs.
† The funnel of a chimney.

lights on the sides, that you may have rooms from the sun, both for forenoon and afternoon. Cast it also, that you may have rooms both for summer and winter; shady for summer, and warm for winter. You shall have sometimes fair houses so full of glass, that one cannot tell where to become * to be out of the sun or cold. For inbowed † windows, I hold them of good use (in cities, indeed, upright ‡ do better, in respect of the uniformity towards the street); for they be pretty retiring places for conference; and besides, they keep both the wind and sun off; for that which would strike almost through the room doth scarce pass the window : but let them be but few, four in the court, on the sides only.

Beyond this court, let there be an inward court, of the same square and height, which is to be environed with the garden on all sides; and in the inside, cloistered on all sides upon decent and beautiful arches, as high as the first story : on the under story towards the garden, let it be turned to grotto, or place of shade, or estivation ; and only have opening and windows towards the garden, and be level upon the floor, no whit sunk under ground to avoid all dampishness : and let there be a fountain, or some fair work of statues in the midst of this court, and to be paved as the other court was. These buildings to be for privy lodgings on both sides, and the end for privy galleries; whereof you must foresee that one of them be for an infirmary, if the prince or any special person should be sick, with chambers, bed-chamber, *anticamera*, § and *recamera*, ‖ joining to it; this upon the second story. Upon the ground story, a fair gallery, open, upon pillars; and upon the third story, likewise an open gallery upon pillars, to take the prospect and freshness of the garden. At both corners of the further

---

* Where to go.   † Bow, or bay, windows.
‡ Flush with the wall.   § Antichamber.
                ‖ Withdrawing-room.

side, by way of return, let there be two delicate or rich cabinets, daintily paved, richly hanged, glazed with crystalline glass, and a rich cupola in the midst; and all other elegancy that can be thought upon. In the upper gallery, too, I wish that there may be, if the place will yield it, some fountains running in divers places from the wall, with some fine avoidances.* And thus much for the model of the palace; save that you must have, before you come to the front, three courts; a green court plain, with a wall about it; a second court of the same, but more garnished with little turrets, or rather embellishments, upon the wall; and a third court, to make a square with the front, but not to be built, nor yet enclosed with a naked wall, but enclosed with terraces leaded aloft, and fairly garnished on the three sides; and cloistered on the inside with pillars, and not with arches below. As for offices, let them stand at distance, with some low galleries to pass from them to the palace itself.

CPSIA information can be obtained
at www.ICGtesting.com
Printed in the USA
LVIC06n1407110618
580315LV00031B/1051

9781163002889